30 Days of Inspiration
"From the Sideline..."

Kim M. Martin, CTACC

DEDICATION

To my daughters Kristine and Kathleen. My angel here on earth and my angel in Heaven. To my parents John and Marie Martin, my sister Christine Miller, my brothers John C. Martin, III. and J. Alexander Martin.

I am who I am because of YOU.
You continue to be my inspiration.

To my "circle". You know who you are. Thank you for being my strength and encouraging me to stretch beyond my limits and step fully out of my comfort zone.

To Jerrod. Thank you for loving me unconditionally.

You all complete me. I love you infinity!

CONTENTS

ACKNOWLEDGMENTS

I wish to personally thank the following people for their contributions to my inspiration, knowledge and help in creating this book: Denise Davis, Denise Terry, Equauler Brown, Tiana Johnson, Clifton and Tavia Allen, Carol Gambrell-Hughes, Michelle Grant, Barbara Miller and Danette Moss.

Without you, this book would not have been possible.

Day 1

Having a strong support system is important as you strive to make positive changes in your life. You want to surround yourself with people who are going to pour into you and provide the encouragement you need to move forward. This is why it is important to evaluate your relationships to ensure that toxicity is not present. Anyone who is making too many withdrawals and demands from you, physically or mentally, will counteract the positive things you are trying to do. Being in the presence of those who can accept you authentically, releases you to make positive changes without fear of rejection. Take the time to assess those people in your circle and make sure that they support you as you expand your purpose and plan.

Day 2

Sometimes it's ok to just "be". Sometimes the "to-do" list has to wait. We all have days when we just don't feel like doing anything! It can be an indicator that our bodies need time to rejuvenate. There is nothing wrong with taking time to recharge. We spend so much time scrambling to complete tasks, make appointments and meet deadlines that we forget to schedule some much needed "me" time. Listen to your body and take the time you need to come back strong. Take a bubble bath, a few minutes to meditate, treat yourself to a cup of tea, or hit the spa….OR JUST LAY ACROSS THE BED AND DO NOTHING! The choice is YOURS. Productivity and success follows when you take time out for YOU!

Day 3

Fear can be paralyzing. It can cause us to miss the blessings and opportunities that are waiting for us.

Breaking the bondage of fear starts with knowledge. Finding out the root cause of our fear releases us to seek the help we need to conquer our fears. Fear is a defense mechanism that was designed to protect us from imminent danger. It was not designed to be a band-aid for our ego or insecurities. Stepping outside of our comfort zone should be embraced, not feared. We have to be willing to walk confidently into situations, understanding that the outcome of our experiences help us to grow and stretch beyond our limits.

FEAR NOT!

Day 4

Being "present" is so important when making positive changes in our lives. We have to learn how to tune out the "background noise" in our minds so that we can be fully engaged with those around us. Sometimes we become so consumed with what we could or should be doing, that we miss opportunities to pour into others and have them pour into us. The purpose of getting together with friends, family, co-workers and other people we meet, is to CONNECT. You can't connect if you don't plug in! So take a deep breath, clear your mind and focus on being present in the moment. You will find that your connections will be more significant and memorable!

Day 5

Have you ever heard the saying, "You have two ears and one mouth because you are supposed to listen more than you speak"? Although amusing, the statement does have merit. We are all guilty of having a conversation with someone where we either cut them off before they finish their thought or we "half-listen" because we are already formulating our response. In order to be effective communicators we have to be willing to listen more than we speak. It opens us up to being better gatherers of information, which will help us create better connections with others. We all have a desire to be heard. We all want our "turn" to speak, but we have to be willing to reciprocate the desire for others to do the same. Being an active listener takes practice, but once you master it, the emotional benefits for both parties are immeasurable!

Day 6

Do you know that you have influence? As you get up each morning and go about your day, you never know who's watching you. You may say something to someone, not realizing that your words were overheard. Your words and body language are constantly being evaluated by those around you. What we do and say can influence someone positively or negatively, so choose your words wisely and think before you act. Remember, your first impression can be a lasting one. Take the time to check your outward appearance as well, to ensure that it accurately represents who you are.

You don't realize the unseen influence you have on others, but know that it is there. It is what draws people to you. Take a look in the mirror and ask yourself, "What kind of influencer do I want to be?" Then walk out the door with the purpose of influencing and inspiring those around you!

Day 7

What recharges and restores you? When you've had a rough day, who or what centers you and brings things back into focus? It is so important to make sure that we do things to pour back into ourselves. We are like a well. When we are constantly being "dipped" into, eventually we "run dry". We want to do things and surround ourselves with people who are going to keep us full. It is a blessing to have this valuable resource, especially when we are going through any type of life transition. Don't wait until you are completely depleted before you recharge. Learn to identify those times when you are feeling a little stress and plug into that resource that restores you. It will help give you the strength to push through and move forward.

Day 8

We all have a story to tell. Whether we choose to keep it personal or down the road choose to share it publicly, journaling is a wonderful way to record the events that take place in our lives. It serves as a reminder of the things we have overcome and victories we have experienced. Negative experiences can remain at the forefront of our minds. Sometimes we forget about the good days and the blessings that have taken place. If you are a journal writer, take time to read through the pages of your past. They will remind you of where you came from, where you're at and where you're going. If you are not a journal writer, consider giving it a try. No one can write the events of your life better than YOU. It's your story…

Make it a best-seller!

Day 9

Connecting with positive people and watching them flourish and grow is the best "reality television" in the world. The news covers enough of the negative things that are going on around us. Take time today to tell someone who you have watched mature or who has made an impact the lives of others, that you are proud of them. We should be about the business of encouraging each other for the positive things we are doing in our communities and in our own homes.

Real life… real talk.

Day 10

When it comes to relationships, whether personal or professional, please remember one thing…everything is okay until it's not! While things are amicable with you and the other party, take time to establish parameters and set boundaries. Draw up contracts and agreements that outline what is being established. Be clear about your expectations and what is expected of you. Seek legal counsel if necessary, to ensure that you know your rights and are protected. Being proactive in your business affairs and affairs of the heart will avoid unnecessary grief and financial loss in the future.

Day 11

Our lives are "Subject to Change". No matter what situation we are currently in, we have to understand that it can change. We will make errors in judgment and we will make mistakes. But we should take comfort in knowing that we can change things for the better. We also have to understand that change takes time. When you take on the mindset that your life is subject to change, then you can release those things that are preventing you from moving forward. You don't have to be "stuck". Expect and embrace change. With change comes empowerment and growth. The question is… Are you ready to make a change?

Day 12

As women, we can spend so much time trying to please others. If you are a "people pleaser", don't you realize that one of the people you should be trying to please is YOU? It is okay to want to please others, as long as it doesn't lead to animosity because you feel "slighted". Take time out to do things you enjoy and that bring you satisfaction. The time you give yourself is the greatest form of self-love and self-worth. When you are filled and restored, imagine how much more willing you would be to please others.

EVERYONE wins!

Day 13

Do you have CSN syndrome? That is when you "Can't Say No"! In our effort to please others, we feel obligated to say yes every time someone asks us to do something. We have to be careful not to say yes to things we honestly can't or don't want to do. It can lead to feelings of bitterness, especially if the request compromises our time or takes more effort than we anticipated. It is okay to say no! Saying no releases you from the obligation and any negative repercussions that could occur had you said yes. We sometimes create situations for ourselves that simply could have been avoided had we just been honest with ourselves and others. Don't add more to your plate than you need to. Remember, even on a plate, it requires that the meals be BALANCED. Balance your time and energies by not overextending yourself. JUST SAY NO!

Day 14

Brendon Burchard's book, the ***Motivation Manifesto*** says these words, "Choosing our own aims and seeking to bring them to fruition creates a sense of vitality and motivation in life. The only things that derail our efforts are fear and oppression." Powerful words! Once we realize those things that give our life purpose, we should feel a push to move forward without abandon! The revelation alone should let you know that some form of action needs to take place. We can't let fear or oppression capture the free spirit that we have been given. Seeking to live a life of purpose requires inner strength and a willingness to change. Don't allow yourself to be derailed. Stay on track and stay the course. Where it will take you will be beyond your dreams!

Day 15

When you choose to make changes in your life, a shift takes place. The desire to move or act in some way becomes overwhelming. When you release the kickstand on your life, it allows you to move. As you are moving, be fearless! Let faith be your helmet and your circle of friends be the knee and elbow pads you need to protect you, should you stumble or fall. You are covered! It all starts with the release. Are you willing to move?

Day 16

As you are rediscovering your passion and purpose, remember to always have a plan. Even if you are not sure where you are going, begin to organize where you are. Having a plan for where you are gives you clarity as you discover where you are going. Putting things down on paper and visually assessing them allows you to weed out those things that may be causing delays and blockages in your journey. Remember that plans can change as future items manifest themselves. Change your plans accordingly so that they align with the path you are following. You will find that a well-developed plan will be the key that unlocks the doors of rediscovery.

Day 17

Aspire to inspire. Think of the person who inspires you the most. What makes them an inspiration? Are their characteristics ones you would like to follow? As you transition and grow, aspire to be an inspiration to those who may be watching you. It may be a child, a family member, a friend or a co-worker. You never know the impact you can have on someone's life by the manner in which you carry yourself. It is a blessing to know that you can inspire others as they have inspired you. Be willing to pay it forward.

Day 18

It is great to have a vision for your life. More importantly, you have to be disciplined enough to carry out that vision. Discipline in fulfilling your vision should be a joy, not a chore. Without discipline you are creating restrictions on your vision. Be a willing participant in following your vision and watch how it manifests itself! It all begins with discipline…

Day 19

Time is not promised. Once the day is done and the dawn of a new day comes, that time is lost. It can never be retrieved. We should always strive to make the most of the time we are given. Each day should be an opportunity to learn or experience something new. Our connections with people should be long-lasting and meaningful. We should seek joy and purpose in all we do, so no time is wasted worrying or harboring hate. What are you doing with the time you have been given? Waste not!

Day 20

I always tell my friends that 'work" is a noun and a verb. It's where I go and what I do. But it goes a step further. If I want to have a successful business, I have to be willing to work at it. If I want to have a successful relationship, I have to be willing to work at it. If I want to reach my goals and aspirations, I have to be willing to do the work. It is more than where I go and what I do. It's how I grow in all areas of my life. That requires a strong work ethic as well. What kind of "worker" are you?

Day 21

When it comes to making decisions, understand that each one comes with consequences. Those consequences can have lasting effects. When making hard decisions, think about how those decisions effect not only you, but others. Think about whether you can live with the consequences of your decision, especially if it cannot be easily changed. Decisions should never be made in haste. Time should be taken to research the information surrounding your decision to ensure that it is made based on all the facts you can gather. So often we allow others to force us to make decisions we are not ready to make. This is when you have to be willing to say that you need time to make that decision and be reasonable about how much time you will need to respond. If time is a factor, ask what the consequences would be, should you change your mind. If it is just something you are not sure about and there may be too many variables involved…just say NO. It is okay to want to be sure before you make a decision. It is your life and your responsibility to make sure that you are doing what is best for YOU. The ultimate decision is yours…

Day 22

In order to live a life that is authentic and transformative, we have to be honest with ourselves and others. Has someone ever asked you how you were doing and you said, "I'm fine". Did you really mean it? How many times have we masked our pain and emotions in an effort to not have to talk about it or to give the appearance that our lives are without issues? It is understood that we don't want to discuss our personal issues with everyone, but we also want to make sure that we don't avoid addressing them at all. To be authentic, we have to be able to validate our feelings. If not for anyone else, we should validate our feelings for ourselves. Once we do this, we can address our issues and begin the healing process. It's okay for things not to be okay. We are a work in progress. Instead of saying, you're fine, say how you really feel. Try it and see how it will free you!

Day 23

When was the last time you took a long hard look in the mirror and examined yourself? The shape of your face, your eyes, the curve of your mouth, any freckles or other identifying marks you have? What you are looking at is uniqueness. You are fearfully and wonderfully made. There is no one like you. When you look in your eyes, do you see strength, confidence, sincerity, or fear? Your eyes are a reflection of your soul. What do you see? Do you see history? Do you see the future or the past? What do you see? When I look in the mirror, I see Love. Value. Self-worth. Purpose. Experience. Growth. Hope. I aspire to inspire. So the next time you look in the mirror, see who you are AND who you can be. When you look at yourself with love, you will see that you are more than meets the eye…

Day 24

Aja Brown, the youngest Mayor of Compton, California was featured on a panel discussion at the 2015 Hope Global Forum in Atlanta, GA. When asked about who inspires her, she said that her mother was her greatest inspiration. She always told her that there wasn't anything she couldn't do. Aja then said these profound words, "If you don't get invited to the table, make your own!" What inspiring words and a call to action! We have to be willing to go into unchartered territories in order to blaze the trail for others. Sometimes that requires us not waiting for permission to do so. Are you a trailblazer?

Day 25

Kat Cole, founder of Cinnabon, said these profound words when speaking about women's roles and advancements in the workplace: "Just because you have a seat at the table, doesn't mean you have a voice." You may have been given a position as a board member or you may be the only woman or minority on an executive team. The question is, were you given this opportunity because of the value you bring? The "table" you choose to sit at should be representative of what you believe in. More importantly, if you find that the organization or group you have committed to does not allow you the opportunity to express your thoughts and opinions openly, then you may want to reconsider your "invitation" to sit at that table…

Day 26

We have to be careful not to give people authority over our emotions. When we allow negative words to penetrate through us, we give that person undeserved power. When we allow anger or a lack of self-worth take root, we feed those negative words and actions until we become paralyzed by them. We allow those words or actions to cause us to doubt our abilities. We begin to believe that they are true. Don't give anyone that much authority over your life! Let their words roll off of you like beads of water. Don't let them penetrate into your spirit and keep you from walking in your destiny. Smile and take the moral high road, knowing you have value and worth. Our blessings come when we learn not to let others dictate our emotions and devalue who we are. Know your worth.

Day 27

Removing clutter from your life produces the clarity you need in fulfilling your vision. Decluttering restores order. Take time to periodically declutter your life so that the path you are on is clear, both physically and mentally. Do this until it becomes habit. This way when true obstacles come your way, you are better equipped to handle them.

Day 28

When we reach a point in our lives where we feel like things are just "status quo", what should we do? It may be a good time to explore our interests and expand our minds. Whether it be continuing our education, reading, exercising or engaging in a hobby, we should always be looking for ways to grow ourselves and stretch beyond our limits. We will never know what we are capable doing if we are not willing to explore new things. We want to be careful not to become sedentary or complacent. The more we pour into ourselves the more vibrant our lives will be. What haven't you tried yet? What are you waiting for?

Day 29

Dictionary.com defines a defining moment as "a point which the essential nature or character of a person, group, etc. is revealed or identified". A defining moment is a time when something about yourself, that you may or may not have been aware of, is brought to light. A defining moment shapes you and allows others to see who you are authentically. The most important part of a defining moment is being able to identify it. We have to make sure that we are in tune with ourselves and that we have aligned ourselves to act when a defining moment is revealed.

When your defining moment comes, will you be ready? How will it change the course of your life?

Day 30

"Where are you?" This is a question you may have been asked several times in the past. You are asked this question when someone wants to know where you are physically. Today, I'd like to ask you the question from a different perspective. Where are you EMOTIONALLY? Where are you SPIRITUALLY? Where is the AUTHENTIC YOU? When was the last time you checked in with yourself to see where you are? Maybe it is time to take out your personal GPS to find the answer to these questions. It's time to give your life the DIRECTION that it deserves. It is time to transition into the calling on your life.

Are you ready?

UNLIMITED LOVE AND LIFE COACHING

"Breaking the Boundaries of Love and Life"

Visit our website www.unlimitedloveandlife.com

Like Us on Facebook www.facebook/unlimitedloveandlife

Follow Us on Twitter www.twitter.com/loveunlimitedco

Follow Our Blog Talk Radio Show
www.blogtalkradio.com/loveunlimited

Kim M. Martin & Sheronda L. Barksdale are
Life Empowerment Coaches, Authors and
Professional Speakers
They are the Co-Founders of Unlimited Love and Life
Coaching, LLC and the Co-Hosts of the Blog Talk Radio
Show, "Love Unlimited: Relationship Coaching
with Kim and Sheronda"

Visit their website to schedule your coaching session, workshop or
public speaking engagement TODAY!

Visit www.amazon.com/author/kimmmartin
to purchase my latest books online

www.ingramcontent.com/pod-product-compliance
Lightning Source LLC
Chambersburg PA
CBHW070750050426
42449CB00010B/2409